CALIFORNIA STATE UNIVERSITY, SACRAMENTO

This book is due on the last date

D0397660

14,00
60

By Harvey Mudd

Soulscot (1976)
Stations (1980)
The Plain of Smokes (1982)
A European Education (1986)

HARVEY MUDD

A EUROPEAN EDUCATION

Black Sparrow Press ■ Santa Barbara ■ 1986

A EUROPEAN EDUCATION. Copyright © 1986 by Harvey Mudd.

All rights reserved. Printed in the United States of America. No part of
this text may be used or reproduced in any manner whatsoever except
in the case of brief quotations embodied in critical articles and reviews.
For information address Black Sparrow Press, Box 3993, Santa Barbara,
CA 93130.

LIBRARY OF CONGRESS CATALOGING IN PUBLICATION DATA

Mudd, Harvey   1940-
   A European education.

   1. Europe—Poetry.   2. Holocaust, Jewish (1939-1945)
—Poetry.   I. Title.
PS3563.U33E8   1986   811'.54   85-22840
ISBN 0-87685-659-8
ISBN 0-87686-660-1 (signed)
ISBN 0-87685-658-X (pbk.)

Photographs by the author.

for Max Finstein
1923–1982

"Untersuchen was ist, und nicht was behagt."

Goethe

PROLOGUE

Among my earliest memories (I was born in 1940), I find the "experience" of the Holocaust. These are not actual experiences, of course, but emotional ones that came to me via the overheard conversations of adults and, perhaps more powerfully, from the images that appeared immediately after the war and during the Nuremburg Trials in the pages of *Life* magazine—images which have indelibly marked my consciousness. Because of this marking (which has excluded me to some degree from life's simple joys), I have long felt the need to make the facts of the Holocaust, at least intellectually and emotionally, my own. Therefore, in the fall of 1979, I embarked on a journey into that history, a spiritual (and literal) journey which became my experience of the "European Education."

I began the journey in libraries. From books, survivor accounts primarily, I learned simple things.

That, for example, such normative concepts as "civilized" and "sane" are a sham, for the Holocaust, as paradigm, appears to manifest an undeniable truth about Man, a truth that manifests itself with such regularity that it must be considered to fall within the range of the "normal." It is the same truth that is declared by the Soviet Gulag, the Kampuchea of the Khmer Rouge, Soweto, and, quintessentially, by the penetration of thermonuclear weapons into all areas of our political, social, and psychic lives.

9

And, for example, that our language, which clings to such archaic metaphors as "savagery" and "bestiality," lags in its evolution behind the 20th century permutations of human reality. The difficulty of making meaningful, by which I mean truthful and accurate, discourse about human nature and the meaning of these events seems almost insurmountable. But is, therefore, all the more necessary.

More than lives have been lost in this cataclysm (though I doubt that there is anything more terrible to lose). The theological metaphor of Hell has erupted from the depths and become actualized in the Death Camp. It is a Hell that differs from the Dantean metaphor by being, by orders of magnitude, more terrible, and by being devoid of any moral purpose whatsoever—here it was not the guilty who suffered, only the powerless and the unlucky.

But what could I add to a story that has already been told in such harrowing detail by those who actually experienced it? Did I, in attempting to speak of it, commit, out of the need to examine and heal myself, a sort of sacrilege, an arrogation of lives and deaths that were not mine for a personal process whose end I am still not clear about? Should I add only silence, some private act, to the suffocating layers of almost unbearable testimony that cover, like the ash that buried Pompeii, the mass grave?

It is the grave also, I firmly believe, of Western Civilization. That civilization, which I am a part of, which I had believed to inform the World and whose values I believed I lived to advance, has been incinerated in the furnaces of the Holocaust.

What life stirs in those ashes? Shall any new form of human life emerge from them? Who am I that I live a relatively "normal" life amid such devastation? Who must I be to continue to live at all?

10

The need to speak, therefore, even if I spoke only of a failure to understand, remained. So, in January, guided by Goethe's admonition "to investigate what is, not what pleases," I set off by boat and train for "the East." What follows is a record, then, not of the Holocaust

. . . but of personal experience within the landscape of that history, a Journey

> through geographies
> of ignorance and denial
> to events unquestionable as the flows
> of basalt and ash that sprawl,
> like the tentacles of the Apocalyptic beast,
> below Etna and Vesuvius.

> To speak of History
> allows the pretext that the forces
> that we speak of sleep.
> Time, behind itself, has merely cooled,
> leaving the terrible formations
> of What Happened.
> Down-slope, at the creeping fore-edge,
> is the hot flux of the present,
> the convulsion that becomes
> What Happens Next . . .

A European Education

A dull torpor of mind has made me vegetate for the last three years. Perhaps, busy in my garden, in daily contact with the plants, I have taken on their habits. The least sentence costs me an effort; . . . at the least suspicion of a thought, some cantankerous critic, always hiding deep in my mind, would rise to ask: "Are you sure that it's worth the trouble to? . . ."

The trip to Germany last summer shook off my apathy somewhat; but as soon as I got back here, it took a deeper hold on me. I accused the weather (it rained incessantly that year); I accused the air. . . . The fact is that I was becoming stultified; no enthusiasm, no joy.

Andre Gide, *Journal*, 1904

Episode I

MYSELF: PSYCHOLOGY

While Berlin rose
I lay for an hour in the bed
without courage or direction:
an hour which became an aimless week.
I worried unnecessarily about my health;
I berated myself for laziness and sensuality
and worldliness, a despair
which unfairly riddled
a relatively moral and conscious life.
And I dreamt, full of sweating self-pity,
of dying young,
as if there were some figure,
myself presumably,
suffering, acting, loving,
that I had still to render
in enduring colors on a plaster wall.
A wall, which even as I worked,
became a ruin.

I had no entry to the labyrinth
I'd set before myself
(half-old, at forty),
or that the world had,
until, in *The Journals*,
which I read each night,
I observed how Gide transformed
the actual, however insignificant,
into cohering possessions of the mind which served,
like tactile landmarks in a cave,

to guide his psyche
into deeper understanding of itself,
and into more sure engagement
with the world.

I turned, thus, the stalled first page,
and acknowledged on the second
that I attempt this epic
into the obscene, the dreadful, and profane
that I may, somehow,
heal the spirit-wound it's given me
and thus end the wasting of my life-force,
as I often have, withdrawing
from what could nurture me,
and scattering myself,
a self-wounding, across sterile pleasures,
or into these fields of ash.
Yet to tell the story,
I must enter as participant,
as a man acknowledging the crimes of Man.
To enter it and emerge whole,
as I hope to,
I must open some deep vein,
as slaughtering a complacent bullock,
and let it bleed.

In, thus, the divided kingdom of the two Berlins,
I begin a journal record
kept in a green book, in pen.

It is no longer a matter of restoring ruins, but of building anew on a ground that must first be tested. Everything must be questioned, doubted again; nothing must be accepted but the authentic.

Gide, *Journal*, 1931

Episode II

BERLIN: TOPOGRAPHY AND ARCHITECTURE

Both cities, this January,
are black with soot
and white with snow
and irreconcilable.
In the west, concertinas of barbed wire
scroll like frozen cirrus clouds
around the ruined Kaiser Wilhelm Chapel
which is now memorial
to the "martyred evangelists" of the war.
There is no mention of the other dead.

The city perseveres,
yet deceives itself about the nature
of its illness: blaming "geopolitics,"
it has forgotten that it was divided
from within. In the city guide,
a single line dismisses '39 to '45
as a period when Civilization
fell somewhat into disrepair,
as if the Assembly Hall of the Great
White and Christian Fraternity
had developed in its roof a few minor leaks:
—during the second war,— it says,
—the city was heavily damaged
and is now rebuilt—.

In this thin soil of poor remembrance
the weed graffiti flourishes:

in English, Kill the Shah,
in Arabic, a call for Holy War,
and in the native tongue,
Jesus ist tot,
the Son of Mary, dead.

From the East, as on a little wave,
comes propaganda, refugees,
and diesel smoke from the slumbering
Soviet panzers: a flotsam that washes up
against the rebuilt West,
its palaces of commerce and pleasure,
its towers of steel and glass.
In victorious neon along the Kurfürstendamm,
the names of the economic engines
that drove the machinery of *Weltkrieg*:
Porsche, Siemens, IG Farben,

Mercedes-Benz,
whose three-spiked star
revolves over the city
like the tantric wheel which,
ascending, delivers riches,
but descending,
reclaims all it gave
in death.

I have always had more understanding, more memory, and more taste for natural history than for history. The fortuitous has always interested me less than the necessary, and it has always seemed to me that one could learn more from what is repeated every day than from what occurs but once.

Gide, *Journal*, 1921

Episode III

GERMANY: GEOGRAPHY

Today I crossed over into East Berlin
where I saw healthy men and smiling women,
so it can not be hell.
Though it's harder to enter than hell is.
But it's drab,
so it's not heaven either.
It is simply half of a divided world,
like all the rest of it.
And the little I can know of it
will be directed by internal baffles
(a distrust of Germans, my gender
and sexuality) that hang
like distorting mirrors
in the corridors of language
I move along.

But I work to refine a method.
I seek in the involuntary stirrings
of the muscles that support the soul
indications of What Matters,
and of these take measurements
which I record as images:
it is a way of knowing which is,
perhaps alone, capacious enough
to permit talk of everything.

Still, each image is the reflection of myself;
my understanding moves only when I move.

And I can offer only the partial:
as this snapshot of myself
(evidence only
of the intelligence I invoke
to aid the education of the heart),
standing in the European cold
before the statue of the great German geographer
Alexander von Humboldt,
who mapped the unknown (which was,
before he went there, only legendary),
studied volcanoes and their effects on climate,
charted the shifts of the magnetic pole,
and late in life, his "improbable
years," as he called them,
attempted to understand the Whole.

The statue is supported by nymphs and pans
whose marble faces and genitals
have been corrupted by the acid rains
of the two Germanies.
Von Humboldt stares down at the marble exemplum
of his great work, *Kosmos,*
whose structure he envisioned,
with the uninjured spirit of the 19th century,
as endlessly and encyclopedically
expandable. I envision
a vicious and encircling history
that devours its own tail . . .

And what I essay here is modest,
but difficult:
a description of self and process
struggling, like a sparrow
in a net, against the grid of history,
which processes me.

To describe the world
within the geography of the cosmos
is ambitious, but simple:
it is the Middle Zone between Heaven and Hell,
where perfection and chaos
have arranged themselves
into the real and the inescapable.

... everyone has the adventures he deserves; and for choice souls there are privileged situations, special sufferings, of which vulgar souls are simply incapable.

Gide, *Journal*, 1921

Episode IV

EUROPE: HIEROLOGY

There is no better study
of who we are
than what we do with life in the body
and with the body of love,
which are among the few sacred possessions
that remain to us.

*

I have returned in the night on the *S Bahn* to *Zoo*.
Then beyond the bustle and glitter of the Ku-Damm,
I follow the guttering candle of my own torments
into the heart of the beast.

At the Klub Minos
I watched a lady with mottled aryan flesh
impale herself on the stiff black phallus
of a muscled and chained Nubian,
(a theatrical that evolves
from Leni Riefenstahl's discovery
that the life of other creatures,
races, sexes, could be rendered into product
and used like a neuroleptic
to stir a goose-step in the loin or mind);
then she, the dominatrix,
in black rubber and gas mask,
performed a *sonderaktion*
with a one-legged man whose stainless steel

foot she took, a dead thing
glinting in the footlights, into her womb.

And I, like a man bewitched,
turned swine and in private bondage,
prayed for mercy, until she,
this Hecate at the crossing of two dark *Strassen*,
released, with her gloved hands
like a fist around each penis,
these mere animals, the flecks
of semen, like volcanic ash,
scattering on the black rubber of her mask,
on the mouth-piece and the lens.

And I dreamt, on my narrow bed,
that on that same stage, I met
the naked figure of the master/
and/mistress of ceremonies:

—*Meine Damen und Herren,*—
terrifying, she,
full breasted, beardless, male,
lapis and silver at her throat,
hair the color of oxblood spilled on sand,
and beautiful as understanding is
if we transform,

—*Damen und Herren, danke,*
for participating
in the dream that we perform
and you command.
But be not alarmed,
for though we mirror the fearful spirit
that rules Men,
when we appear to hurt, we don't.

But we do not feign the truths
of who we are and what we do.

Now I who, as female and male combined,
guide all mortals who would escape the slum
that lies between Heaven and Hell,
remind you as we close our hall,
that the daylight world outside
is unnaturally partitioned
into *Ja* or *Nein*.
But here anything is possible,
and you will not feel so much
the violence of a mind
divided against the heart,
if you'll remember that tomorrow night
we return to this small stage,
where everything that can be imagined
will be performed,
yet remain confined. —

It is not at all that I feel more "human" today than at the time when no trace of such preoccupations could be found in my work. I simply took care to forbid them access to it, judging that they had nothing to do with art. I am no longer sure of this, nor that anything can and must remain foreign to art; it runs the risk of becoming, it necessarily becomes, artifice if what is closest to the artist's heart is banished from it.

Gide, *Journal*, 1931

Episode V

THE WEST: PATHOLOGY

Berlin by day is grey concrete
and full of people.
It seemed that no one here
had ever caught the plague of War
and died of it.
I wandered for hours among ordinary lives:
soldiers, tradesmen, and housewives,
dogs and pigeons.

And I searched in my own life
for something evergreen,
a memory of love or beauty to protect me
from thoughts of suicide
and the fear of failure
that would, I knew, beset me
as I journeyed beyond Berlin
and deeper into the understanding that I sought —
or would, perhaps, be blessed with
and receive,
as one does history,
or one's life,
or the last disease.

I searched also for the Plotzensee,
the suburban prison where the failed plotters
against the Führer were tried,
were tortured, died.

*

Beyond the skeletal forests of the Tiergarten,
near the wall, an old soldier,
hair disheveled, a leg gone, crutched
grotesquely, like a raven,
amid the frozen trash, the while hurling
evangelistic rage into the hazy air;

and, twitching like a marionette on a wire,
he jerked his arm upward toward the polluted sun.
No one paid him the least mind
except the pigeons, who scattered,
making patterns in the sky
(which I try to read), who remembered
how that motion usually punctuated
the rant of hatred

that infected millions of ordinary men
with the desire for power
that swims like a blind microbe
within each servile and helpless soul,

men whose self-loathing
turned on the powerless,
slaughtering them to give Power its meal,

and making of the offal a bloody culture
that spawned the flattering monster, Destiny,
and his dreadful twin, the State.

And finally as this brief
oracular pattern in the flight of pigeons
(as if the word he used, — Gott, —
were the clap of thunder) dispersed,
I found behind the public Krankenhaus
where the terminally ill shuffle about
in their grey bathrobes, already ghosts,

Episode VI

MYSELF: MYTHOLOGY

In the Savigny Platz,
in rooms over *Das Grune Baum Kabaret*,
an interlude:

I was at first terrified of her
who had only consorts,
old men who, like enchanted dogs,
brought food and clothed her in fine clothes,
and whom she rewarded kindly
(but only as one does a dog),
as she strolled each night
among the tables of her smoky temple
singing Schubert and Kurt Weill,
terrified of the beauty of her voice,
that I would adore also
and be kenneled in Berlin forever.

But one night, I held the terrible history
of the German people against her,
as a sword to heart, and she wept,
confessing nothing,
for she had done nothing,
but was still ashamed.
And I was ashamed for what I'd done,
and I wept for her, and for myself;
and I confessed myself
a co-conspirator in the guilty history of Man,
though I too had done nothing.

And I stayed with her three days.
And we clung to each other,
like swimmers in an unnamed sea
whose depths drop suddenly away,
to each other and to desire,
and did not drown.
She taught me landmarks for the journey,
essen, lachen, suchen,
eat, laugh, seek,
and words for parts of the body
and the heart.

And in the late nights, while the *S-Bahn*
sped past on its satin rails,
we became as two creatures, gentle
and speechless, joined in what seemed love.
Though she, perhaps more innocent than I,
remained apart, serene
as the full moon that presided over
our winter union in Berlin—
a moon that illuminated briefly
my obsession with a world
where merciless hunters
pursued exhausted animals who spoke also
the language of humans,
Deutsch.

—*Liebe,*
mein jüdisch Liebe—
for she thought me Jewish,
so mindful of rituals for the dead,
remembering them,
and of rituals for the living,
hanging her underclothes by the gas flame
that they be warm after,
careful with the *samentötende,*

the word she taught me that my seed die
and not return as a half-Jewish revenant
to remind her, in the fall,
after I'd crossed back
into the crimes and torments
of my own *Ausland*.

A constant need of reconciliation torments me; it is a failing of my mind; it is perhaps a good quality of my heart. I should like to marry Heaven and Hell, *à la Blake*; reduce oppositions and most often refuse to see anything but misunderstandings in the most ruinous and fatal antagonisms.

Gide, Journal, 1937

Episode VII

THE WORLD: SUMMATION AND EQUATION

Have we enough devotion to our own lives,
to the faithful cells whose attempt at unison
makes each of our lives possible,
that we'll pause, loving
those cells, and by loving,
number them, and by numbering,
remember each of the six million dead?
And is shame enough
that we will be permitted into
the presence of the unremembered
and offer them,
if not the gentle comforts of revenge,
at least apology?

I, for one, fail of such devotion.
I am too impatient.
And my personal experience of shame
is too inconsequent.
I confess, for instance,
a moment of bad behavior in a public washroom,
pulling rank (read race and money) on a Pakistani man
over who'd use the toilet first,
(I bowel sick and not at my best).

And Original Shame,
that sorrowful murmuring
that whispers along the spirals of the helix
and translates into the revulsion that I feel
at being born a man

in an age when Man has so implacably
revealed himself as belonging to the party
opposed to Life's purpose,
is too abstract to carry much baggage
for the endless shuffling columns
of the dead.

No, shame is not enough.
The victims, perhaps embarrassed by
or even contemptuous of this effort,
remain hidden behind the gathering rubble of human time.
In the actual present someone spills current blood
before we know and count the dead.
And most of us know them only faintly,
on the evening screen or morning page.

Today, 18 January, I decipher
in *die Frankfurter Allgemeine*
a narrative of the *Kambodisher* Boat People:
of men who were thrown alive
into the shark-grey sea by Chinese pirates,
of women who were then raped by the same pirates
with their children looking on,
(one pictures, with narrative distancing,
which I too can not avoid,
gestures of distress and fear that have,
against the backdrop of wide sea and cloudless sky,
a mannered eloquence,
as figures on a fan or parlor screen),
of the same *Kambodishers*, fewer now,
who were set adrift again
to be captured next by Viet pirates
who raped the women a second time
and who threw next the children
into the now death-cloyed sea,

upon which still sailed Thai pirates
who raped the same women a third time.

Rescue seldom happens,
but does often enough
that we know these tales.
Some of the women, I'd guess,
will cross grief's sea, remarry,
raise children again.
Marvelous creatures, humans!
How durable!

And how predictable
is the misproportion of their lot and luck
in the Middle Zone:
much torment and suffering,
much, as many torments
as the leaves on a thousand willow trees;
but little justice, a rare root
which, in the rubble of Berlin,
I dug for traces of.

* *

Beyond the now deserted Potzdammer Platz,
the old Times Square of the *Reich*,
is a field, surrounded by tank traps and wire,
its ruins cleared, that no one owns.
Snow covers the mound of earth
that is the remains of the *Führer* Bunker
and the still-murmurous pile of ashes
that was the bodies of Hitler,
Eva Braun, Goebbels, his *Frau* and *Kinder*,
bodies which were baptized in gasoline
and sent heavenward (meager hecatomb),
as the Red Army drew closer.

At which the Dark Instigator shrugged,
drawing back into his vent
in the volcano's bowel.
—Time's over for this one,—
he said, philosophical,
—but there will be others.—

      * * *

I feel a bit the fool,
or at least a primitive
like the ancient Irish bards
who threw their incantations
at monsters and bad kings
hoping to destroy them.
And I'm easily as unsuccessful as they were,
attempting here
to imagine a punishment adequate
to satisfy this crime.

But I must attempt it.
I cast at the memory of evil
this curse
which falls, I know, short:
still, let this particular soil and ash
be mixed with sweepings and shit,
with metal filings so that all rust,
and then splintered
into the smallest most inconsequent
particle; small,
small
may his memory become;
yet may his *Geist* live unconditionally
forever, somewhere
beyond the Einsteinian Heaven-edge,

where, freed of time/space,
he may not ever wake from,
must ever wake into,
the most phobic terror he had while living,
whether such is being entered from behind
by a dark man with earlocks and hooves,
or having his stars cross,
or his stomach knot
so that his bowels not move
forever.

This I, knowing the limitation of speaking, an impotent
stammering, utter beneath my breath,
lying on my bunk, which is moving
within and across time/space,
on the *Nachtzug* to Warsaw.

         * * * *

From the window, I see the half-moon
shine on the ice fields of no-man's land
and glint on the coils of wire
that demark frontier.

And I think of the singer,
whose acceptance of the creature that I am
gave some proportion to me,
and freed me from the cage
of being merely Western Man.

The history of the past is the story of all the truths that man has released.

Gide, *Journal*, 1894

Episode VIII

WARSAW: ARCHAEOLOGY

I was oppressed by the ravens
of Warsaw. They are heavy creatures
that rise, carrion and garbage filled,
on wings that flap like the black sails
of a ship that brings the plague
or terrible news.

The crescent moon is like a shovel.
I use it to remove the lyric overburden,
the effluvium of language
that is produced by floods of feeling,
but which contains no thread of story
that we may follow
while descending along the steep way.
In proportion to the gravity
in the depth of things, a simplicity
that must approach silence.
There is no analogue, however,
to the silence of the underworld
more accurate than silence itself.
In this, still I fail.

Today, I went to the Umschlagplatz,
the rail-head from which the Jews of Warsaw
departed for "relocation" beyond the Bug River,
a place where, the Death's Head Official said,
—Jews eat better than Poles do.—
I eat nothing today.

I follow the rail lines,
120 kilometers north and east of Warsaw,

to what is surely the saddest ruin on earth.
Treblinka, in the snow,
in the pine woods.

Here, the fragile shelter of civilization
which humans erected
on the surface of the lava flow,
the State, purposively, with flame
and ideology, has begun to disassemble.
Here, living children were dismembered
or thrown alive into the firepits.
No structure remains except that,
the coliseum of fire, a pit, under snow,
a kilometer long, 50 meters wide,
15 meters deep. In it
the individualities of 800,000 people
were disposed of.
What remains are their emotions
held like a frozen murmur of voices
in the strata of time and icy air.
I excavate as deeply as I dare:

their dread of death coming;
their dread of the physical pain;
their rage at the injustice;
their humiliation at their impotence;
their shame of their nakedness;
their grief for themselves;

their grief for their children
and for their line;
and, finally, their horror,
discovering

that what had once spoken to them
from the burning bush
was both God
and Not-God,
was both revelation
and mere flame,
that the revelation was extinguished,
and the flame consumed.

Worse things may have happened to humans,
but what they might be
I can not uncover.

. . . If upon opening that door I were suddenly to find myself facing—well, the sea . . . Why yes, I should say; that's odd! because I know that it ought not to be there; but that is a rationalization. I can never get over a certain amazement that things are as they are. . . .

Gide, *Journal*, 1924

Episode IX

AUSCHWITZ: GEOLOGY

At Auschwitz-Birkenau
I found no trace of emotion.
Here everything is reduced to the physical.
This is the Louvre of Death
and there are only specimens and fossils.

I must preserve myself,
yet observe and record faithfully.

There are rooms
of tens of thousands
of dentures and eyeglasses,
of shoes, black, desiccated, and unpaired,
of toothbrushes and shaving brushes,
of battered, labeled suitcases,
—Anna Marie Cohen, Den Haag, Holland,—
of thousands of artificial limbs,
arms, legs,
a room of crutches.

I smoke foul black cigarettes,
injuring myself, as if embarrassed
to be healthy, clean, and literate
amid such loud evidence
that the aspirations of the human spirit
will reduce to such silent rubbish.
And that our evolutionary failure
was caused by an over-density of the masculine,

a black hole within us that draws into it
everything Life allows us to dream of.

In the depths of Auschwitz
sorrow
is metamorphosed into nausea.
And metaphysical horror
becomes the gag-reflex,
but under such great pressure
even that instinctual flight from danger
fails.
Here I experience a monotony of dread
that inspires no reverence for the dead.
This is Death's deepest kingdom
where the dead are dead utterly
and the heart is oppressed utterly,
is without voice,
or courage.

Glass and explanatory text in Polish
intercede between us and the specimens.

There are rolls of woven haircloth,
and matted uncarded mountains of women's hair.
There is a Hall of Children:
in the glass cases are babies'
clothes, dolls, rattles, tiny
wrinkled shoes, bottles and nipples,
a Polish Mother Goose.
There are thousands of prayer shawls
hung on wires, becoming
as a curtain on a stage behind which
there are neither actors,
nor plot, nor author,

only the corridors that lead
to the rooms where they slept so closely,
in cribs and on the floor,
that, racked with dysentery,
they had to walk on the bodies of their fellows
to find the slit trench,
or shit on them.

Along the corridors of the barracks
are photographs by the SS:
the faces of doomed men and women,
their heads shaved, ears protruding;
(the faces of young women etch most deeply
into the mind of this memorial).
Their eyes stare with terror
at the figure of Death behind the camera
as He prepares them, poses them,
then reveals the naked obscenity of his hatred,
as he prepares to rape their souls
and exterminate them.

Only memory resists.
Throughout Auschwitz this winter
there are red carnations.
On the glass cases, the gallows, the doors
of the furnace, on the iron tumbrels that plunged
each voyager into the silent levels
below the bottom of Hell.

. . . I reread the fifteenth chapter of the Gospel according to St. John and these words are suddenly illuminated for me with a frightful light: "If a man abide not in me, he is cast forth as a branch, and is withered; and men gather them, and cast them into the fire, and they are burned."

Gide, *Journal*, 1916

Episode X

KNOWLEDGE

And always at Auschwitz in those years
there was loud music,
circus and parade music,
never German music,
which was prohibited.
The band played on the platforms
as the transports unloaded,
played to drown out the noise
of chaos and terror,
the crying of mothers and children,

and to muffle the silence
of the Vatican,
the Red Cross,
the White House,
Number Ten Downing Street,
the Government of Poland in Exile.

Though never
did the music cover
the sighs and coughs of their sleeping,
the moaning in nightmares
that were pleasant fictions
compared to the reality which dawned always
with the shouts of the SS,
—*Alle Juden raus,*—
the dull thwack of truncheon on flesh, —*raus,*—
into the cold or the heat

to be selected each day
by a twitch of the finger of the doctor,
for work, *rechts,*
or for death
in the dark showers beyond the wire,
links.
And the band played to celebrate
the elegance of a formula which multiplied

the failure
of Christian Civilization
(X)
by the cruelty in Man
(X)
by the networks of rail across Europe
(=)
to yield this cipher, the perfect nil,
(0)
Auschwitz.

Verhalten Dich Ruhig.
is scrawled in red letters on a barracks wall.
    Be calm and silent —
And a terrible Silence is what I heard
in these vast wired precincts
that once contained a machine whose noise of process
drowned the music of the spheres.
This was a great city once,
whose citizens all died in service of an industry
whose one product was Death.

In the plaster walls of the showers,
the scrape marks of finger nails,
and the marks of children's nails

lower on the wall:
a mannered eloquence,
as figures on a screen.

In the next room, the furnaces.
One escaped
only through the chimney.

It is through man that God is moulded. This is what I
feel and believe and what I understand in the words: "Let man
be created in our image." What can all the doctrines of
evolution do against that thought?

Gide, *Journal*, 1916

Episode XI

KRAKOV: COSMOLOGY AND ARCHITECTURE

In the Jama Michavel cafe
the piano player plays love songs.
The Polish intellectuals sit
in threes and twos discussing Iran
and Chopin, Solidarity which rises in '80,
and Singularity, that which occurs
only once in the universe.

Auschwitz is not Singular.
It is the evolved paradigm
of a chronic disease in Man,
a disease whose live virus we observe
swarming like maggots
out of the present evidence.
The disease is found
nowhere else in the universe.

These are a few of its terminal symptoms:
9mm high-velocity bullet in the neck's base,
enforced exposure,
exhaustion,
beating,
800 calories per day,
6000 volts in the wire,
noose,
medical experimentation,
the gas zyklon B.

From these I have escaped physically.
I have the treasure of life still
and expend it today to wonder
which of the tortures that preceded death,
terror,
hunger,
pain,
humiliation,
or filth,
my spirit would have succumbed to.
As I have no doubt it would have.
Probably the filth.
And the discovery of what Man is.
And the decay of ideas
I thought imperishable.

Though Auschwitz-Birkenau,
like all the great tombs of history,
will not decay.
Its architecture is as majestic as the pyramids.
Two million worked to build it,
gave their last breath of devotion,
gave themselves cinder upon cinder.
And though it is flat and nondescript
and no longer populated, it has
a cosmic form, Smoke,
that still orbits around the world
and shrouds the climate
in which we raise our children
and into which their children
will be born.

Nothing illustrates my thought better than this cynical and wonderfully ferocious remark of Valéry, so eloquent "in the domain of the absurd." It was a long time ago. We were young! We had mingled with the idlers who formed a circle around a troop of wretched mountebanks. . . . They were admiring a poor woman, thin and gaunt, in pink tights despite the cold. Her team-mate had tied her, wrapped her up, skilfully from head to foot, with a rope from which, by a sort of wriggling, she was to manage to free herself. Sorry image of the fate of the masses; but no one thought of the symbol; the audience merely contemplated in stupid bliss the patient's efforts. She twisted, writhed, slowly freed one arm, then the other, and when at last the final cord fell from her, Valéry took me by the arm:

"Let's go now! She has ceased suffering."

If one fails to understand the irony, the tragic beauty of this remark, it's a pity.

Gide, Journal, 1935

Episode XII

MYSELF: ALCHEMY

The dead, at last, appear to me,
in sleep. And a spokesman comes forward,
an old man with an earring
who resembles Max. He lectures me,
as he did often when alive.

—History is an illusion,— he says,
—for all that has ever happened,
and will happen
in a single event
of equal and infinite parts
past and future.
Though, for those caught in the cattle chute
of a terrible present,
it can be exhaustingly narrow
and slow.

The world is a cabaret in the Middle Zone
where What Happens is performed.
Here, by the command of Gravity itself,
the Created
and the Acts of Man
come together to perform,
though not in unison,
still as One.

It is the grandest of the *Grand Guignol*
and it's had the longest run in town.
But its meaning, which you've sought

while wandering in these slums,
eludes, and will until
you change the methods that you use.
The mind, which you've put
your entire weight upon,
leads, like the great lizard's size,
to a tar pit in the future
called Dead End:
And you, the Men,
are the worst offenders,
demanding that the world rearrange itself
into what you dream.
You have stubbed your toe at last on the stony fact
that the world is already that.
And what the world is
is who you are, and that
is what the world means.

Within the perimeters of this truth
you must learn to live.
And it will remain your prison,
a *Konzentrationslager* for your soul,
until, within yourself, you find a gentler truth;
that, not Work or Power,
will make you free.

But now, the forgetting you condemn in others
begins in you.
This is mortal and excusable.
For we, the dead, are dead forever,
and are as nothing.
You will become as nothing
if you think too long
on what does not exist.

Yet we are still,
and will transform, as you shall,
for as long as you remember us.
And while you live,
we desire that you do. —

"The true scholar is he who is able to find in experience perhaps a reply to what he was seeking, but also to listen to the reply to what he was not asking"; who accepts considering even what he did not expect to see, were it to surprise and embarrass him considerably.

Gide, Journal, 1930

Episode XIII

VIENNA: BIOLOGY

I awoke Sunday
in approximately the Perfect Republic.
I saw a man burning his only flag on a rooftop,
and fell in love that same night
with a beautiful girl
who was rebaptized each day of the week.
—Today I am the moon,— she said to me
on Monday. You see how it is here?

We spoke of the animals, how alive
they are faith-filled,
but dead, are disillusioned and incurable.

But enough sadness,
it is the return voyage.
I am a sailor in taxis
in a city without alliance or schism,
where automobiles flow centrifugally,
like words whirled by a wind from a speaking bush:
—Wonderful,— it says,
—Life is activity,
and the dead are still.—

And here there are laws against loneliness
and sorrow and aging,
though nobody obeys them.

I held her on Tuesday,
in our attic sailboat that floated on traffic noise,

noise like the waves of a bottomless ocean
booming and receding.
—The only part of me, *mein Liebe,*
that is virgin
is my toes.
And I would sell them also.—
And I bought them,
and was happier than I had thought possible.
Each toe was as lovely as a blossom.

—What if in a week's time
I have a sore?—
I asked her.
—Think of Job,— she replied,
—he was covered with sores
and still he loved.—
You see how it is?
I could have stayed forever.

Today it is Wednesday.
I wear the mask of a Worldly Man
and tell interesting lies
about what I have done, and what seen.
—There are,— I tell her,
—lovely women of pure marble
who hold up the lintel of heaven,
and pyramids of ash
that contain the Treasure and Nothing.—
She is wide-eyed, amazed.

I deny any knowledge of myself,
and of the Princes who partition the world
into the Kingdom of Life
and the Kingdom of Death,
for such ideas are difficult
and we are resolutely simple.

I say nothing
about the elusiveness of true love,
for she is doing her best.

Her friend Wolfgang
wears elegant women's clothes
and is the concubine of the Sun King.
Her friend Gretchen wears
a gentleman's tuxedo at midday
and labors at counting the seeds
in the Cosmic Jar.
My love wears the mask of a goddess
and is absolutely the truth.
We two are the first man and the first woman,
who could repopulate the world
if we chose.
We four sit in the cafes
drinking coffee *mit Schlag*,
eating unimaginably luxurious chocolates.
We watch the snow fall,
a beautiful arras behind which is everything,
love, spring, and the past.

She says to me,
—You don't have to be pure or intelligent
to get into heaven, which is here.
To the east is the empire of the Turk,
to the west is Napoleon.
We Viennese are in the middle,
have beautiful carpets and profiteroles,
and it is heavenly.—

On Thursday her dog died.
She cried in my arms,
cried tears unimaginably round,

perfectly proportioned with sorrow and salt.
Here, only life is imperfect.

—The imagination,— I tell her,
—is the place of understanding,
and we must visit the temple.—
It is unfinished,
or in ruins, which I can't tell.
Its architect was lost in a camp,
or, some say, run over by a trolley.
We go on Friday.
They sell souvenirs by the construction site:
wax hearts,
lead models of the great edifice,
figures of the god Irony to put on the mantel.
We are asked to contribute.
There is a machine
with stereoscopic views of the world.
For a small coin, views,
l'tombe, l'livre, l'volcan,
and some others, all unreal.

And we visit the house of Mozart.
There is no music in the bare rooms
and no heat.
But Mozart is immortal,
is seen daily in Vienna,
at the *Konzertgebaude* tapping his baton,
or screwing his wife under the piano.

And we visit Freud's house
where on irregular days
Gods still congregate,
the fat ones and thin ones,
the cheerful ones and the sulkers.
Freud too is immortal,

though he sleeps through this visit
by Eros. She sits in the anteroom,
polishing her nails, while I marvel
that any man could read so many books.

I hold a snapshot of her,
my sweet Friday.
It is blurred,
though in the background
the structure of the unfinished
is unmistakable.
I am afraid that when I leave
the snapshot will dissolve,
as the wafer does in the mouth
at communion. —You are
more beautiful than the Host,—
she once said to me, as I too dissolved.
You see how generous she is,
how wonderful and ordinary,
almost unbearable.

On Saturday, I sail again.
I have the treasure to deliver,
my journal of ashes.
I call it News of the World.
My true wife, whom I scarcely remember
or whom I've never met, waits.
I will never see my Viennese girl again.
Just as well.
The body is a great luxury
when there is so much to know
and to do.

—There are gods and citizens and creatures,—
she said to me,
—and we two are divine creatures.—

We have labored 4000 years
to come to this.
So nearly perfect.
A Law against the Rule of Man
is the last thing we must conceive of,
and in the Congress of Creatures,
give birth to.

To love the truth is to refuse to let oneself be saddened by it.

Gide, *Journal*, 1940

Episode XIV

MYSELF: HISTORY OF CONSCIOUSNESS

A long train ride through the Tyrol
to Venice. The panic subsides.
And as I ascend into these calmer regions,
I remember how,
at 20, from a stone house
on a hillside above the Guadalquivir
I had embarked, with the ambition
only the young are capable of,
on the study of the architecture of the cosmos.
I read the Quijote
and listened to Vivaldi and Bach
on a phonograph that played,
like the salt mill under the sea,
as if it would play forever.
The "Gloria" of Vivaldi
and Bach's Third Suite for Unaccompanied Cello
were the only music I heard for a year,
and within their ineluctable logic
the entire man-made and created universe
seemed contained.
The landscape outside seemed equally purposive,
the grids of olive groves that surged
and fell over the brown hills toward Jaen
like the formulas of space/time
rendered earthly and beautiful.
In the afternoons, I waded
in the sun-drenched shallows of the Guadalquivir,
whose narrative concludes in oblivion.

And I debated which, music
or river, was most true.

Nights, however,
were hellish in that house.
Cold spewed out of the stone floors
like fumes from sulfur vents
in the sides of Mt. Etna.
It was lonely,
inhabited by rats and ghosts,
neither of which one encounters much in America.
On the stairs once I met
a slaughtered man whom I did not know.
Gore erupted from a deep wound under his heart,
and he held in his right hand his eyes,
as if to say there was something
he had not seen,
or would not see.
This figure came one night only.
In the morning, with the Vivaldi again circling
on the record player, and the orange groves choiring
with song birds, I banished him
to some conveniently Freudian circle,
and continued to wonder how my life study
could reflect
the whole structure,
la Gloria che penetra il universo.

The results since
have been as this is:

tragic, occasionally comic,
discursive, disharmonious,
stressed almost to weeping by my inability
to confine calamitous truths

within the little theater
of word and mind.

★ ★

A bell, monotonous,
on the tidal surge in the channel,
a warning of rocks.
—There is no returning
along the way you've come.
And sleep well.—

★ ★ ★

Morning in Venice comes early
with the sound of workmen removing
old plaster and bricks from a church wall.
Clatter of rubble into a steel barrow.
But I have awakened
with a stubborn feeling of a small joy,
a feeling that comes when something
we have hoped for, but did not expect,
is granted us.
For me it is the beginning of release
from the man I have been.
And the realization
that to understand our own meaning
within a Greater Architecture
was never possible, for we live and die
within the confinement of ourselves,
in a forgotten region called the world.

And that the best we can manage
is to protect our shelter against the fires
that Man brings, to illuminate its walls
with evidence of who we've been,

and to love our fellow inmates,
the creatures with whom we share these barracks,
this Grand Palace that preserves the memories
of the Dead and the Incurable.

* * * *

Faded velvet, the color
of an ancient feminine luxury,
on the walls. Cupids
in a mildewed froth of gilded clouds struggle
on the ceiling over us. I crane my neck
to see the Marriage of Heaven and Earth
by G. B. Tiepolo, and the Allegory of Wisdom.
The colors are faint after four hundred years,
and the west wing of the palace
is slowly declining into the Adriatic.
The sinkage is irretrievable.
My heart flutters at times,
a fortyish physical occurrence
that reminds me of the necessity
of redrawing the maps
as each island of consciousness
sinks back into the uroboric sea.
In the basement, under a splendid
but artificial firmament,
the receding stars rendered
by glass chips in a black stuccoed field,

is the sacred *Tesoro*,
which is also the Eternal *Niente*:
the tooth of St. Agnes is here,
a piece of the shin bone of St. Dominic,
a bit of hair and ribs

from the martyrs of the siege of Constantinople.
And here, encased in silver and worked lapis,
the colors of the night sky,
is the brown and desiccated head
of St. James the Younger.

Stress now.
My pen digs into the paper.
My friend has had her breast removed
(her breast discarded);
a cobalt implant
has burned her flesh from armpit to plexus,
and chemicals have destroyed
her memory for books
and conversations and history.
But she is, she hopes, cured,
and has come to Venice,
which is a city of continuous memory,
to celebrate
and to find something to remember.

We talked in those March days
of home: hers, Chartres;
mine, America;
of spouses, hers; mine, none;
of children, books, death camps, and disease;

talked over wine and octopus,
talked as we studied
the frescoes in the dank palaces,
as we watched the silk peeling from the walls
and the empire of damp invade
the now meaningless books.
Merveilleux, she exclaims over and over.

And I loved this woman, delighting
in how joyfully she took into herself
this crumbling city,
its dark history
of plagues, princes, wars and martyrs,
its present danger
from the sea within it,
and in how, in the crucible of the love
she felt for each day she lived,
she transformed it into blessing,
a labyrinth that yielded at every turning
memory, understanding, pleasure.

* * * * *

In broken Italian,
I asked the old man in the guard's uniform
the significance of St. Sebastian
who is pierced by arrows,
and who dies in the renderings of the 15th century
in an agony which seems almost pornographic.
I expected the simple,
as — submission to God's will, —
or perhaps a more sophisticated,
— history produces martyrs —;

never expecting that he,
half drowsing on his three-legged stool
before a serene Madonna by Jacopo Bassano,
would gesture toward the canvas of St. Roque,
who points to the plague pustule in his groin,
and say, if I heard correctly,

— Because, *Signore*,
arrows, like plagues,
exist in the scheme of things
to violate what lives. —

Pigeon mutter,
like leaf rustle, in the piazza.
The males follow the females
strutting the creaturely hope.
Dogs couple also in the piazza,
within sight of San Marco.
In the animals we watch
the first divine act of the *Commedia*.
The male dogs are especially comical.

We wandered today in the city,
through narrow alleys,
smelling sewage,
passed the gas works
and the central lock-up
and the geriatric hospital.
Took a *vaporetto* to the island of the dead
and Pound's grave,
cleared ivy,
stole a carnation from Stravinsky
who had too many,
and Pound none.

Returned finally to the Rialto.
Savored the smell of fish,
and the smell of the Adriatic.
Marked the pale beauty of squid and shrimp,
irrefutable evidence of the creation,
in white pine crates.
A barge full of ceramic toilets
passes by Santa Maria de la Salute
where we two, amorous and cancerous,

will go tomorrow
for the remission of sins.

Now we sit in our overcoats by Vivaldi's chapel.
There is no warmth in the sun.
The problem of perspective was solved here,
as were the problems of harmony
and public sanitation.
We are capable of all sorts of talk,
can think in allegories which reveal
the many faces of what is Singular.
We will learn our place in the allegory,
a wisdom that will cure
neither terminal disease,
nor hope, nor sorrow.

We have loved with a tenderness
that burns reason to ashes,
and have not died of it.

Thanks to the Blessed Virgin
the bubonic plague is contained,
no longer propels
its dark galley past San Giorgio.
The *Lazzaretto Nuovo* on its island
falls into ruin.
As does the world,
where we two stroll arm in arm
remembering what we dare to.
We are both dying,
but today are almost joyful,

imagining the gentler human
that Man may still become.

Three Short Poems

DEVELOPING INFRASTRUCTURE

Forty-four railcars of dead souls
stand in the Berlin Hauptbahnhof.
They are open backed to the rain,
in plain sight of the passengers
who wait for the Paris train.

The dead souls have been quarried
from the historic ash pits of Poland
and will be consumed in cement
for the extension of motorways
and the expansion of airports.

I am not speaking about the holocaust,
but about sources of raw material,
and about the development of consciousness
and highways in the real world.

A LAST SUPPER

for Thadeuz Borowski
and the others whose tales
of the Holocaust I follow . . .

There is a soup pot in my house,
and into it things fall from heaven.
Potatoes usually,
and once, when we were hungriest,
a white onion fell into it.
A beautiful onion,
concentrically layered,
the paradigm of Onion.

I listened a long while
while the onion wept Kaddish
through the bubbling of the soup.
The bones of a lamb and a pig
wept also in the soup pot.

Thadeuz came to supper.
We divided the bones,
the lamb bones to him
because he perished,
and the pig bones to me
because I didn't,
and because for me
pig is clean.

Then we opened the onion,
historically,
each layer containing
a million stories
that have not been told.
At its center we found a scroll
that revealed the future of the world.
But it was so small
that it would not unfold.

I am indebted to the French novelist, Romain Gary, who first used the term "European Education" to describe the events of this century. I am grateful also to Anna Walton, March Kessler, Gabrielle Lopez-Watermann, Dennis Hamel, Murray Mednick, and especially Judy Chicago, all of whom made valuable suggestions regarding the text.